For 8 year olds who love football

Illustrations by Dan McCloskey

First published in Great Britain in 2023 by Bell & Mackenzie Publishing Limited

BELL & MACKENZIE

REALLY FUN

FOOTBALL FACTS

For 8 Year Olds

Get ready for trivia overload! Bursting with fantastic football facts and amazing stats about the beautiful game.

Which Premier League Striker was born on Halloween?

What's the record for the most red cards given in a match?

Which world class player has a museum dedicated to him?

Which stadium created more noise than a military jet on take-off?

Keep reading to find the answers to these and loads more really fun footie facts...

In Colombia there is a team named Club Deportivo Los Elefantes (The Elephant Club).

The team's logo even features an elephant kicking a football!

Crystal Palace FC are known as The Eagles.

Before matches they used to fly a real live eagle called Kayla around the stadium. Fans would cheer and 'coo' at Kayla.

Zlatan Ibrahimović is one of the best Swedish players of all time.

He has played for six clubs that have won the Champions League, but he has never actually won the trophy himself.

In 1966, the World Cup trophy was stolen just a few days before the tournament was due to start in England.

It was eventually found by a dog named Pickles.

Pickles became a national hero and was even given a special collar with the words "World Cup 1966" on it.

At only 17 years old, Jude Bellingham scored his first Champions League goal in 2021.

This made him the youngest-ever English player to score in the competition.

Fans love the unpredictable FA Cup.

One of the biggest FA Cup upsets was when Wrexham, a non-league team, beat Arsenal in 1992. It was a huge shock for everyone and showed that anything can happen in the FA Cup.

When Ronaldo starts a match he always steps onto the pitch with his right foot first.

It's a Portuguese custom 'entra com a direita' which means to 'enter with the right'.

'Cuju' was an ancient Chinese sport that was played over 2,000 years ago!

People kicked a ball made of animal bladders into a small net, just like in football today.

Player substitutions were introduced to the English First Division in the 1965–66 season.

Substitutions were introduced so that players who are tired, injured or not playing well can be replaced by fresh players.

The fastest footballers can run at a top speed of around 30–35 km/h.

Manchester City's Kyle Walker is one of the fastest ever, clocking a top speed of 37.802 km/h. That would break the speed limit in some streets in cities and towns!

Pelé won three World Cups with Brazil in 1958, 1962, and 1970.

He was the youngest player ever to score a goal in a World Cup match at the age of 17.

Pelé's real name is actually Edson Arantes do Nascimento.

He was known for his incredible dribbling skills and ability to score goals from all over the field, earning him the nickname "The King of Football."

Manchester United won't forget their match against Liverpool in 2023.

They lost 7-0, with four different players scoring!

Penalties were invented around about 1890. No one really knows the exact date.

Before penalties, if someone committed a foul, the other team just got a free kick.

Ever wondered why goalkeepers don't wear the same kit as their teammates?

In 1909 a rule was introduced that goalkeepers "must wear colours that are distinguishable from the other players" so the referee can pick them out easily.

Did you know that pop royalty, Elton John, used to own Watford F.C.?

Although he doesn't own the team anymore, he is still a big fan and was even given a special title as the 'honorary life president' of the club.

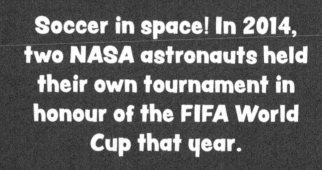

Soccer in space! In 2014, two **NASA** astronauts held their own tournament in honour of the **FIFA** World Cup that year.

The astronauts had to use
special balls and come up with
creative ways to play the game
since they were floating instead
of standing on the ground.

Linesman Andrew McWilliam had an awful day when he vomited during a match between Kilmarnock and Dundee.

The referee then made it even worse showing him a red card – as a joke!

In 1910 Manchester United moved to their famous stadium Old Trafford.

Before they made it their home it was used for cycling and athletics.

Imagine playing a match with so many goals, that the score is 149 to 0!

That's exactly what happened in a real match between AS Adema and Stade Olympique l'Emyrne in Madagascar back in 2002.

The world's highest-scoring goalkeeper is Rogério Ceni. He scored 131 goals for São Paulo FC in Brazil.

As well as being the goalie, Ceni also took penalties and free kicks for his team, which is how he scored so many times.

10 red cards is a record!

A referee in Argentina created a new record for the highest number of red cards shown in a single football match. He pulled out 10 red cards during the Trophy of Champions Final between Racing Club and Boca Juniors, making for a wild and chaotic match.

If you dropped a football from a skyscraper, it would fall so fast it would be going faster than a car on a motorway.

Footballs used to be made of leather.

Now, most footballs are made of synthetic materials like polyurethane. This makes the ball lighter and easier to play with.

Footballs need to have just the right amount of air in them so they can work well when they are being played with.

This makes the ball bouncy and helps it move in a way that everyone can predict and understand.

Did you know Marcus Rashford's birthday is on Halloween?

That's proof he was born to score screamers and give defenders nightmares!

The Mexican Wave, also known as "La Ola," became popular across the world during the 1986 Mexican World Cup.

This was one of the first times football fans outside South America had seen this amazing crowd participation.

Argentina's 2022 World Cup victory bus parade in Buenos Aires had to be cut short.

Four million fans took to the streets to see the winning team and tried to climb onto the team bus! The team had to be evacuated by helicopter.

Some football teams have different kits for different weather conditions.

This includes lightweight and breathable kits for when it's hot and thicker kits for colder weather.

In 2010, football freestyler Dan Magness did 'keepy-ups' for a world record 26 hours.

Dan also did an amazing 100-mile charity walk from Wembley Stadium to Old Trafford while keeping a ball in the air.

It's estimated he did half a million keepy-ups during the epic 10-day journey!

Mbappé won the World Cup with France in 2018.

He donated all the money he earned from the tournament to a children's charity in Paris.

Kylian Mbappé was only 16 years old when he made his debut for Paris Saint-Germain.

That made him the youngest player to ever feature for the club in Ligue I.

Diego Maradona was a famous Argentine soccer player. He is remembered as one of the greatest players of all time.

He used his hand to score a goal against England in the 1986 World Cup, but the referee didn't see it and said it was a goal! He called it the "Hand of God" trick!

The Colosseum in Rome was not just a place for gladiators to show off their fighting skills.

It was also used as a stadium for the ancient Roman version of football called 'harpastum'.

The first ever football match on TV was in 1937. It was between Arsenal and Arsenal Reserves, and was broadcast live to the country for the very first time!

This was a big deal and it meant that people all over the world could now enjoy watching football from the comfort of their own homes.

The 'Scorpion Kick' is a fancy and impressive save made by a goalkeeper.

It happens when the goalkeeper jumps up and uses their legs to stop the ball from going into the goal - like a scorpion's tail.

It's not easy to do and is known as one of the most amazing saves a goalkeeper can make.

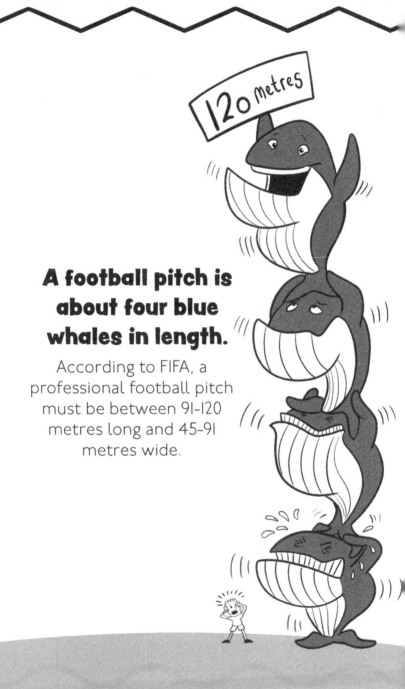

A football pitch is about four blue whales in length.

According to FIFA, a professional football pitch must be between 91-120 metres long and 45-91 metres wide.

120 metres

Football corner flags are placed at each corner of the pitch and must be no less than 5 feet tall.

Harry Kane grew up in a family of Tottenham Hotspur fans.

He has been a fan of the club since he was a young boy.

He even played for the club's youth teams before making his way up to the first team.

He recently became Spurs' all-time top scorer, beating Jimmy Greaves' record of 266 goals.

The offside rule was created by the Football Association (FA) in England in the 19th century.

The rule was introduced to encourage fair play and stop players from just standing near the opponent's goal waiting for a pass.

There is a museum dedicated to Cristiano Ronaldo.

The CR7 Museum in Portugal celebrates the amazing career of one of the best players ever! You can see awards, cool stuff, and learn about his life and impact on the sport.

The average distance a Premier League player covers during a match is 9–12 km.

Can you imagine how much energy and effort these players put in during a match? Some players, like midfielders and forwards, run even more, while others, like defenders, run a little less.

David Beckham is not only a football legend, but also a club owner!

He owns Inter Miami CF, which is an American team in a league called MLS.

Brazilian midfielder and Chelsea hero ' Oscar' became one of the highest paid footballers of all time when he moved to the Chinese Super League in 2017.

He was paid £20 million a year.

That's nothing compared to Ronaldo's move to Saudi Arabian club Al-Nassr in 2022 for £165 million!

Argentinian player Martin Palermo suffered a terrible leg injury in 1999.

He tore a leg muscle while playing for Boca Juniors – but he didn't realise and even went on to score his 100th goal in the league.

The biggest football stadium in the world is the Rungrado 1st of May Stadium in Pyongyang, North Korea.

It has a seating capacity of 114,000 spectators and was opened in 1989.

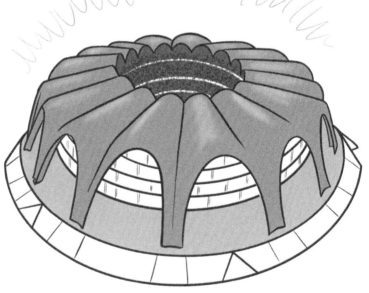

Its roof is shaped like a magnolia flower, with 16 petals made of steel that support the structure.

The oldest football club in the world is Sheffield FC.

It was started in England a long, long time ago in 1857! They still play today and are famous for being one of the first clubs to ever play the sport.

Lionel Messi is one of the greatest players of all time.

When he was a young boy he used to carry a ball with him everywhere he went, even to bed! His family would have to take the ball away from him so he could get some sleep. It's funny to think about a young Messi dribbling a ball in his dreams!

Did you know that when a team wins the Premier League, they get a special medal to take home and show off to their friends and family?

But the big, shiny, original trophy stays with the league.

Referees in some competitions have begun carrying white cards.

Holding up a white card means showing the good side of sports. It's like a big thumbs up to fairness instead of getting a red card for doing something bad.

The most expensive football shirt ever worn was by Diego Maradona.

It sold to a rich fan for over £8 million.

The top clubs have a whole team of people who help the players do their best:

Manager
The boss who tells the players what to do.

Goalkeeper Coach
Teaches the goalkeeper how to stop goals.

Fitness Coach
Helps players stay strong and healthy.

Physiotherapist
Helps injured players get better.

Nutritionist
Tells players what to eat to stay healthy and strong.

Sports Psychologist
helps players be confident.

Wow! Women's football has been around for a very long time!

The first ever women's game was played way back in 1895 in Scotland.

Don't use your hands.

The back-pass rule means a goalie cannot pick up the ball if it was deliberately kicked to them by a teammate using their feet. It's quite a modern rule as it was only introduced in 1992.

Messi is one of Argentina's most celebrated players.

He could have played for Spain, rather than Argentina, if he wanted to as he has a Spanish Great Grandfather.

Did you know that football is played in every country in the world?

It's estimated that over half a billion around the world play football regularly making it the most popular sport in the world.

One of the fastest ever football kicks was by Brazilian soccer player Ronny Heberson.

He managed to kick the ball at 211 km/h in 2006. That's as fast as a high-speed train.

Manchester United legend Mark Hughes once played for Wales and Bayern Munich in the same day!

Some teams are like superheroes! These special "Ever-Present" teams have never been relegated out of the Premier League.

THE EVER PRESENT

Right now, only 6 teams have this super power:

Arsenal, Chelsea, Everton, Liverpool, Manchester United, and Tottenham Hotspur! Imagine being so good that you've never had to leave the big leagues!

Arsenal star Bukayo Saka joined the club at the age of 7.

Looks like 7 is his lucky number, as he also wears the number 7 shirt which was previously worn by club legends Robert Pires and Alexis Sanchez.

A 'clean sheet' in football means that the other team was not able to score any goals during the game.

If a team gets a clean sheet, it means their defence and goalkeeper did a great job keeping the other team from scoring. Three goalkeepers kept three 'clean sheets' at the 2022 World Cup. These were Morocco's Yassine Bounou, Argentina's Emiliano Martínez, and England's Jordan Pickford.

Arsenal's 2003 'Invincibles' are the only Premier League team to play a whole season without losing a single game.

They worked hard, played well together, and always found a way to win or draw their matches.

Man Utd player Christian Eriksen had a really scary experience whilst playing at Euro 2020.

During a game, he suddenly passed out and his heart stopped beating. Quick-thinking medical staff were able to get his heart beating again and took him to the hospital to make sure he was okay.

Did you know that the owners of Welsh team Wrexham A.F.C. are actually famous Hollywood actors?

Ryan Reynolds, who played the Marvel superhot Deadpool, and Rob McElhenney who created and starred in the U.S. show 'It's Always Sunny in Philadelphia' bought the club in 2021. Both were awarded the Freedom of Wrexham in a ceremony in April 2023.

John Burridge became the oldest player ever in the Premier League when he appeared for Manchester City, aged 43 years and 5 months in 1995.

2022 was the Year of 'The Lionesses'.

As well as their historic win at the Euros, the England women's champions also grabbed a bunch of other awards that year.

2022!

Freedom of the City of London

Northwest Football Awards: Billy Seymour Impact Award

T Sport Action Woman Awards: Team of the Year

Pride of Britain Awards: Inspiration Award

Sports Journalists' Association Awards: Team of the Year

BBC Sports Personality of the Year: Team of the Year Award

Manchester City of Champions Awards: Hall of Fame induction

In the old days goalkeepers' gloves weren't as good as the ones they wear today.

They were heavy and stiff and didn't have a good grip or protect the keeper's hands very well.

Nowadays, goalkeeper gloves are made of lightweight and flexible materials that are much easier to move in.

They also have special grips and padding to protect the keeper's hands.

The Türk Telekom Arena held the world record for creating the loudest noise ever recorded in a football ground in 2011, with fans hitting 131.76 decibels.

That's as loud as a military jet aircraft taking off from an aircraft carrier.

Do you know that there's a record for throwing a football really far?

The person who holds this record is called Alireza Beiranvand. He threw the ball over 61 meters when he was playing for Iran against South Korea in 2016.

In 2017 Sheffield Wednesday broke the World Record for the largest 'cake football'.

The giant cake weighed more than an adult lion.

Wanderers F.C. are a team that doesn't exist anymore... but they did something really special!

They won the first five FA Cup competitions. No other team has ever won it five times in a row like they did. It's pretty amazing!

WINNERS
1871-72
1872-73
1875-76
1876-77
1877-78

A 'derby' is a special kind of match where two local teams play against each other.

These teams are usually from the same city and their fans are really passionate about their team. It's like a huge competition between neighbours.

One of the most exciting derbies is the Merseyside Derby between Liverpool & Everton. They first played in 1894 and have played each other more than 220 times since then.

Legendary Manchester United manager Sir Alex Ferguson had royal fans.

During his success at Aberdeen F.C. in the early 1980s he had dinner with the late Queen Elizabeth and Duke of Edinburgh.

Brazilian footballer Ronaldinho lost his expensive sponsorship contract with Coca-Cola® when he was caught drinking Pepsi® at a tournament press conference.

'Awkward!"

The World Cup Trophy is made of solid gold!

It weighs about 6kg, which is as heavy as carrying around 6 bags of sugar. Can you imagine holding a piece of gold that weighs that much?

Nike® Mercurial football boots are the choice of top players like Ronaldo, Neymar Jr. and Mbappe.

They wear them because they're lightweight and help them control the ball really well. So, if you want to play like a pro, maybe you should try them too… but start saving!

Football around the world.....

In **America**, it's called **"soccer"**.

In the **UK**, it's called **"footie"**.

In **Spain**, it's called **"fútbol"**.

In **Italy**, it's called **"calcio"**.

In **Germany**, it's called **"fußball"**.

Did you know that the most footballs that can be juggled at the same time is 5?

That's a lot of balls to keep in the air at the same time!

English striker and national treasure Peter Crouch has several nicknames.

Mostly called just 'Crouchy', he's also known to fans and media as 'RoboCrouch' and 'Mr Roboto'. He first performed his robotic dancing celebration following his goal for England against Hungary in 2006.

A total of 8 countries have won the FIFA World Cup. These countries are....

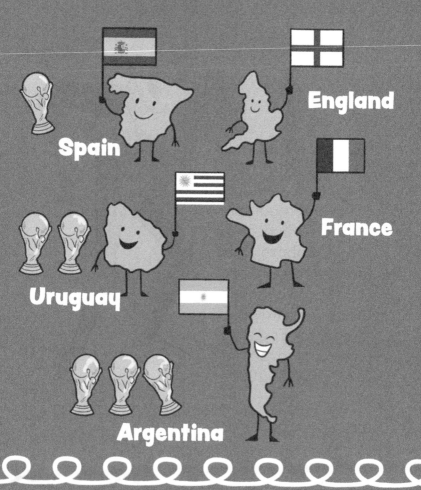

Spain

England

Uruguay

France

Argentina

Brazil are the most successful team in World Cup history, lifting the trophy an amazing 5 times!

Italy

Germany

Brazil

In a 2010 match against Barcelona, Arsenal hero Cesc Fábregas broke his leg.

Amazingly he still managed to score a penalty in the same game!

Also in the Really Fun Football Series.
Collect Them All!

Made in United States
North Haven, CT
20 November 2023

44303172R00055